Stories Concerning

Strangers

THOMAS COOPER

MILTON & HUGO L.L.C.
4407 Park Ave., Suite 5
Union City, NJ 07087, USA

Website: *www. miltonandhugo.com*
Hotline: *1- 888-778-0033*
Email: *info@miltonandhugo.com*

Ordering Information:
Quantity sales. Special discounts are granted to corporations, associations, and other organizations. For more information on these discounts, please reach out to the publisher using the contact information provided above.

Library of Congress Control Number: 2025909225
ISBN-13:   979-8-89285-385-9   [Paperback Edition]
                  979-8-89285-386-6   [Hardback Edition]
                  979-8-89285-384-2   [Digital Edition]

Rev. date: 05/02/2025

Fake poems about real people I've never met and likely never will.
Perhaps you know one or two of these characters.
Perhaps even, one of them is you.

Dedication

To the Ramily that inspired my first-ever poem
And to the angel and the devil on my shoulders. Brock, who
pretends every poem is a masterpiece, and Braden, who makes
fun of every one. Thanks for keeping me in the middle guys.

PART

I

Everyone has a story
worth telling

Talking While Dancing

Stand right there don't move
I like the way the light hits you
I wanna capture you right now
I wanna hang you in the Louvre

Girl I love your style
Coolest girl I've known
The fit's always running hard
You're always running wild

What about you then there?
Al see a mirror for once
Your hair's between groomed and trash
But it unceasingly makes me stare

Dancing like a fire
That's what I'd call your eyes
Burning my clothes off and pulling me
Into both of our desires

That's not what I'm thinking tonight
Don't you know by now?
Just put your vape back in your pocket
And give me your hand to dance till light

Remember when you got pissed
That I didn't know your eye color?
It's not that I wasn't looking
But they're clouded by beautiful mist

Shut your stupid face
You've spent weeks or maybe months
Coming up with that line, boy
— I'm inspired by your grace

Remember when I quit drinking?
— No, when was this?
It's cause I get drunk off you
The world around us is shrinking

Don't say that Sue
— no it's good because
Well. I hate the world and all that's in it
I hate everything but you

What about our friends?

Oh I do love all of them too
But I could lose them each and every one
As long as you stay with me till the end

Keep your arms around me Sue
Hold me through the song
Hold me through the night
And by the way your eyes are blue

A Mommy Loves Her Baby

I don't remember when I was born
I used to think that was a shame
But holding you right now
Helps me understand the why and how
I'm sure my mother held me the same

My mother always told me
Don't grow up too fast
Precious moments do not last
Finally now I really see

When I was a little girl
My mother always tucked me in
Beautiful bedtimes stories to listen
She'd run her hand through my curls

I'll read to you those nighttime scenes
But this is the best one of all
It's about the first time I heard you bawl
When I first saw you without ultrasound screen

My mother raised me well
She loved me with all she could and more
I'll love you from my very core
This I can already tell

When I put her in a nursing home
When you go to put me in one too
I'll hold hands tight with both of you
And we'll never be alone

Holding you in my arms
You sweet little tiny human
A glow from your face illuminates
Saving us from darkness and harm

Your eyes are closed dreaming maybe
Fast and far asleep
This room has silence deep
I love you my precious baby
Tonight I hold my heart

Grow Old Together

(Featuring Al & Sue)

Let's grow old together
Don't laugh I'm serious
I'm sorry it's just so random
Like maybe if u were drunk on brand rum
I just think we make an excellent tandem
Like look at us, you and I

Sue stop what you're doing right now
And just look around the room
Like we could do anything we planned
We could rule this town this land
—*WE COULD START A BAND*
Okay that would be pretty sick

But stay with me here I wanna say things
Well actually I guess "stay with me here"
Yeah that pretty much sums it up I guess
Baby you're rambling u looked pressed
Sorry it's just you're getting undressed
L-O-L I'm just taking off my bra

Plus you've seen me a hundred times
But you haven't lost your beauty yet
You always shine you always glow
One day I won't anymore you know
No, Sue, I don't think so
And that's what I mean let's find out

I wanna stay and age with you
Here look, feel your hand in mine
Never let that connection sever
Feel the warmth of my palm forever
<u>Sue let's grow old together</u>
Sue it's you and me

You really mean this don't you?
Yes I do and also can I hit that?
My pen, Al or hit this ass?
Just let me hit it I don't need your sass
Wow look at the change of class
Fine here you go, you were saying?

Girl you know what you mean to me
I really hope I've made that clear
Omma kiss you if u keep talkin' this way
You know I'd never turn that away
But hold off a sec I got more to say
No, you've talked too much it's my turn

Thank God you're cute because Al
You've never been too good for words
Especially words of the heart
But at least you've given it a start
And now it's time for my little part:
I love you beyond my days

I've loved you for almost two years now
Though I still think you're a loser
And I probably will for two more years
I want you forever Al, my dear
But let me make one thing fuckin' clear
I ain't getting' old

And neither are we Al me boy
—Did you honestly just say "me boy"?
We're gonna die forever young
Together we're gonna sing songs unsung
And we're always gonna kiss with tongue
Even when yours gets weathered & dry

See I'm yours till the end of time
And I'm giggly for every moment
If I were a queen you'd be my crown
If life were a bar we'll close it down
And now that we've figured out our sound
Sue, tell me more about this band

Crazy Love

This contrast feels medieval
Or maybe renaissance
The colors fight their battle
Lights drowning from the shadows

See I'm standing in the darkness
And aside from moon and stars
The only light I witness
Comes from your bedroom window

I'm standing silent on your street
And the only sound is rustling trees
As asphalt lays beneath my feet
Glass pane guards all sound

I can get it through my brain
But carrying hemoglobin's already hard
I can't make my blood also carry pain
Can't get the info into my heart

And my calendar says that time has passed
Leaves change color and decompose
My heart hasn't healed as months elapse
But standing here, I'm outside of time

I wonder what you're doing in there
Listening to your shitty music
Messing with your beautiful hair
I just wish you could hold me, and me, you

And I guess it makes me crazy
I should've moved on by now
My thoughts are getting hazy
I wonder what it meant to you

But then someone talks about us
Makes me think that we were something
And that only makes me start to rust
And I can't keep my feet from melting

So fuck it, maybe I've lost my mind
Maybe I've really gone crazy
But I can't help but feel frozen in time
And all I can think in front of your house is

I miss you

Only Candle

My parents often call and ask
Wonder why I stall the task
The search for career and life
Something to avoid shear strife

But the truth is hard to tell
I'm covered in shards and shrapnel
From the grenades going off
This charade is blowing poff

And amidst all the confusion
From chaos stems resolution
I can't hear the thoughts in my mind
Except the one that says you're not mine

And I'm stumbling around in the night
Concoction of sound while lacking light
The darkness makes me very scared
And I'm here in flakes but I don't know where

You are my only candle
Shining, holding, stand still
All I know is dark surroundings
And you offer my heart light confounding

And the doubts in my head vanish
They go away, fall dead standing
The feel of our hands in hand hold
You are mine, my only candle

Scars

This one's a little deeper
I was just sixteen when drew it
When I went and sketched a new slit
Right across my little wrist
It poured faster when I made a fist

It was a bad week that week
That year was rough from the divorce
My mom just kept getting worse and worse
Home was a wreck and I didn't eat
And the girls at school were less than sweet

And this one was right before college
About to go out into the world
And I'm just a stupid little girl
I wanted to know how a palm bled
And I wasn't surprised when I saw the red

The one above my knee wasn't me
I wrecked on my scooter in the street
And skinned myself up on concrete
And I curled up and cried & threw my helmet
& I cursed 4 the very first time but I still bled

But I think my dear the worst scars I have
Are the ones you can't see with your eye
The ones that only come out when you cry
Like this one's from daddy, he broke my heart
& I know u can't see it but it tears me apart

Or what about this one hiding inside
This one here is from my ex
He was the first time I ever had sex
And he told me he loved me, I think he lied
When he cheated & left me part of me died

Scars, scars they're terrible things
But I can see them all in the mirror
Whether they're visible or not, they're clear
And that makes them part of me
Yes scars shape our identity

And the only reason I'm telling you this
Is because I've made room for a new scar
If I confide and you break my heart
At least I will be prepared for the sting
See I'm not dreaming of diamond rings

But I think that I can trust you
Something in my gut screams him
So I'll show you my scars from thick to thin
And I hope you can love them all
Heartache, abandonment, alcohol

Gingerbread Man

Swing low, sweet chariot
Come quick cause I've got places to go
Swing low, rusty Chevrolet
Coming fourth but I ain't goin' home

I was faster than the other kids
When we ran around at recess
Ceaselessly running from my peers
Like a magician I'd disappear

Mom told me to run as fast as I could
So I'd get up and pick up my knees
In Khakis I'd play on the asphalt
Bloody cargo pants but never halt

Growing up, not growing tired
On the first day of grade eight
Late to class met my childhood sweetheart
But sweet turns sour and sweet turns tart

Apparently, she liked my dick so much
She tried three other guys just to compare
Bare on all fours on her dorm room floor
Long distance breakup, she went on to try more

Felt like a cowboy when I got my first car
'92 Silverado, topper and all
Call of the west was ever grand
A knight without armor in a savage land

Got my degree by fingers on digits
Offered by a firm in Puget Sound
Looked around to hell with accounting
Enough on my mind without slipping and drowning

So I fled to the land of the latter-day folks
Spent my weekends admiring Alta
Salt in the lake but none for my sidewalk
Busted my ass when the snow came to knock

But I met you in that snowfell city
Blue-gown grad with a knack for singing
Ringing to this day in my head
Chili peppers, hot and red

Love of my life, however short
I took your heart but not your hand
And ran away like all I know
Can't be caught not even by Provo

The waves south of rainfall pulled me away
San Francisco playing bass guitar
Stars are ugly above that bay
Ship sounds haunt me to this day

The cabbie one night got a d-u-i
My buddy Shawn got impaled
Sailed through windshield and into a pole
I would've helped but I was out cold

And I got cancer later that year
Couldn't even see the tumor
Rumor has it I beat it though
Not that you'd care, or even know

Yeah, I never got tired from playing tag
But as the price of gas constantly rises
Surprises here and there come plenty
Now as of late, I'm running on empty

I hope this letter finds you well
Or rather, doesn't find you at all
Crawling under miles of barbed wire
As no man's land stretches on and higher

I'm heading back to Utah
But only to catch a one-way flight
Might stop for a second to think about you
As the plane carries me far from view

New York City just called my name
And Paris and Prague are waiting in line
Time seems to be my only friend
Not even thirty, so much to spend

Bells will be ringing the glad, glad news
Christmas then New Year's and what done have I
Fly till I catch an Eastern wind tunnel
Bound and down watch me run and run still

Trouble in the Club

Let me sober up a second
I haven't had a lot
Two or seven vodka shot

Tornado round target
Thoughts cycling round
Surely motif-bound

How are you by the way
How was sophomore year
I haven't missed you dear

Lie and lie again
I'll do it more than twice
I really should take your advice

But the place is loud tonight
Loud with light and sound
Emotions scourged and drowned

Get a second round
This buzz is losing hue
Walls collapse in front of you

Scream it to the world
Most nights bring hurt and sting
But fuck, tonight is groping

So fuck those other nights
The ones where I miss you dear
Tonight I'm breathing exosphere

Silhouettes

Fragile thing in my arms
That's what you said to me
My hands were lined with sweat
Your heart was full of blood
And I hadn't lost you yet

You were a thread and needle
Now I'm cut and bleeding
Need for stitches needless worry
Never been one for blood
My sight is getting blurry

You were never one for candles
So we always left the lights on
Our silhouettes held each other tight
They swayed and shuffled poorly
Living off of needed light

Two nights blend together
I stumbled and I fell
Your words were cut and bare
Blood was on my forehead
Sweat runs down my hair

My biggest fear you knew
Of being delicate
I still leave the lights on and twirl
Silhouette with two left feet
Swaying and searching for plural

Bare-Naked Thoughts

I managed to get dressed today
After three days spent in sunlit dreams
You know me, streak-breaker it seems
Just like when I broke our two-year run
But I digest...digress?

Words were never my forte
Just like when I said those words that night
I should've just kept my mouth shut tight
Should've kept my lips together
Maybe later they'd meet yours

Guess what, I didn't drink today
Though that's mostly cause the fridge was clear
Didn't need gas station beer
Guess I was scared I'd be triggered
Remember all those times I had to buy your new vape?

I wonder where we'd be today
Probably be as if nothing changed
High on your couch, laughter exchanged
My head feels tight lately
I'm not sure if I miss you or the feelings you gave me

I'm fucking sorry
What else can I really say
To make these bad thoughts go away
I don't like anything anymore
I just want things to be better and they're not

But I managed to get dressed today
And I'll try again tomorrow
Syllables, syllables, sorrow
Maybe I'll step outside for some sun
And maybe one day I'll get out of the darkness

Big City Enthusiasm

City lights are nighttime stars
That's what she said to me
They twinkle as if to a ship at sea
Millions of bulbs to describe the night
You don't need stars when you have city lights

You don't need mountains I suppose
That's what I said to her with heel
When you can scrape the sky with steel
What's the worth of the highest hill
When we can pierce the clouds with will

That wasn't what I meant at all
Rebuttal ringing clear and true
Glacierborne rivers can still be blue
Even if manmade canals are wide
But that doesn't mean we can't take pride

I think that I am catching on
Take birdsong at the break of day
Street music can be lovely in a different way
That's right and downtown markets built on stone
Like vibrant jungles, you're never alone

People are better than credit is due
And their ecosystems can go wrong
But usually they come along
God made stars but also made you and I
And the stars we make can light up the sky

Legacy

I am Ignatius, a child of Crow
My ancestors hunted buffalo
I am a hunter too for commission
I make sales calls in an office in Michigan
In Baghdad my father killed evil men
I chase lines on a table for adrenaline
Generations of blood come down to me
The latest heir of Cannot See
Corporate share and a 401k
They ask what's wrong but I cannot say

I am a star-maker

He didn't believe her when she told him
That she put the stars in the sky
He only scoffed in his reply
Thinking that it was a silly thing
She insisted she birthed the distant lights
Said she danced on top of the pitch-black nights
She said I am a star-maker
Bend your knee
Confess with your tongue that you're in love with me
But the words of truth didn't carry
They failed to reach his stubborn heart
From his ears it pulsed a lightyear apart

The boy now struggles to fall asleep
He tightens his eyes away from the blinds
As starlight trespasses into his mind
She spins her yarn in spite of him
With pin and thread she sews the stars
With every trace she stitches up scars
She's floating on cosmic dust above
Not weighed down by his gravity
Casting rays out of depravity
The star-maker walks calmly in the sky
Her problems still linger down below
But she picks them up and makes them glow

Heaven by Hangover

I woke up this morning in my king sized bed
Pounding aching spell in my head
Something in this apartment reeks of booze
But I didn't have a drop last night to lose

I sit up and watch the walls and light bend
This vertigo's gotta be some new trend
I see hands on a clock but I've fallen from time
Like raindrop to rooftop I can't find the rhyme

I hear echoes of voices all around
Some singing some screaming sources unfound
From last night to last year the memories blur
I try to speak out but the words just slur

This morning's no different than the last few ones
Months blend together when you've come undone
My monthly deposit surpasses my bills though
A bachelor by degree and an empty pillow

How long has it been since I've come to this place
Ringing in my ears and all over my face
How old am I now 24, 28
Every point from the sunrise to sunset feels late

Where is Ernie my great old dumb hound
Where is my sister and her feet on the ground
I barely remember Mom's warm chicken stew
I barely remember the son she once knew

When was the last time I heard my heartbeat
With will I imagine the sight of my home street
The chains on my wrists and my ankles feel tight
For the first time in forever- I wanna be alright

I gotta do something but what, when and how
If I can stand up then I can leave town
If I can stumble then I can walk
And find the last place where I could talk

I gotta force myself to scream
I feel paralyzed in a hazy, indifferent dream
Something's burning in my chest
A sensation that calls me to venture to quest

My keys on the nightstand my shoes by the door
If I don't leave this instant I'll stay forevermore
I've been here for ages or lifetimes perhaps
I'm so fucking furious at this suffocating lapse

Save me from this desolate limbo, Mom
I'm gonna run and never look back on 'em
Leaving with angels escaping this city
I haven't felt anything for eternity

For the sake of the one (that's fucking me)
I wanna play fetch with good ole Ernie
I wanna hear birdsong in my backyard
I don't want to be salt- cold, coarse, and hard

Leaving my wardrobe and my empty flask
If anyone wants it but I doubt they'd ask
To hell with this vacuum that's pulling me in
I'm trading this king for my childhood twin

I'll run down the highway like a dog chasing cars
I can't be caught by this life of prison bars
I'll climb out this pit and into good feelings
Hug my sister and friends for hangover healing

All Souls Day

Featuring *Al* and Sue

Sit down
Did you just say sit down?
I was gonna say sit down
You were gonna say sit down?

—*Sue.*
Al et tu?
Some things I have to say to you.
I remember when every dream was new
Recently all my dreams are in blue
Of all the things I wish were true
Never did I consider this hue

Fuck.
My lil schmuck
I too just feel so stuck
It's the cold autumn season of the buck
But when you say it too I just-it sucks
Like a skinny needle's numb skin pluck
It seems that we ran out of luck

It's like- remember last Christmas Eve?
We said we'd cut and tear and cleave
But we couldn't force our blood through sieve
Sue all I ever did was believe
I'll ring a somber bell to grieve
It's gonna hurt like hell to leave
And I don't know what's for the best

Do you feel that chill and humid breeze?
Grimly reaping leaves from trees
My bones are cold like some disease
And you can't save me Hercules
So don't even try to. Please Al please
Let us go and let us cease
I really wanted to, you know?

I know my sweet romantic boy
I'll miss this hand on my cheek my joy
Replace it with a pillow
Set face wherever wind will blow
Maybe we won't grow old at all
Die next week from a seventh floor fall
Fuck you don't say things so dark
We're gonna survive we've come so far

I'm sorry Sue I'm just not sure
I was just so certain and now
Now it's like there's no future at all
No present no future
No time itself but the fading past
Ghosts two days after Halloween

...

The lady Evelyn Susan LaRue
With eyes of unforgettable blue
Boy I'll always remember you
Please don't
Oh shoe
Since when have I ever listened to you

The Angel in C-303

Out like a light do angels dream?
I wish you could hear my consciousness stream
Evaporate my thoughts into steam
Don't let them boil up into a scream
Let them condense to a lucid seam
Like dew on your hair under halo gleam

Sweet boy in my arms I hold you so tight
Sunrise brings bad dreams, I seek the night
When neon club signs replace sunlight
My heartbeat races when it comes into sight
When my angel descends from cloudy height
I get the call to come over and it's all alright

Remember when they tried to tear us apart?
Their scheming efforts were a work of art
My friends all disliked you right from the start
Thinking your cheating was something tart
But they just didn't know my angel's heart
Choosing you over them was more than smart

Lend to me your wings that I may fly
That I may join you up in the sky
I'll float to your floor three stories high
To seduce me you don't need to try
Intimately look me in the eye
Lasting moments to make my heart sigh

Your smile is like a solar ray
But for some reason my world is gray
I'm somewhat scared I can't see the way
It's okay that your forgot my birthday
I hope you know I want you to stay
For my angel to just feel the same I pray

Safe in your apartment C-303
Light seeps through the window so eerie
My guardian dear may other girls flee
I only want you to only want me
My angel so pure and kind and free
Flow my consciousness stream to the sea

the end of the world

Thinking about you tonight
Yes, tonight of all nights
I suppose it's a mix of a multitude of things
Like the humidity on my porch before the rain
Like the smell of the trees gifted by the wind
Or maybe it's the end of the world.

Do you remember all my drinking?
God I was such a mess
I couldn't go a day without it
Summer and winter blurred
I fucking the Fall
And I miss the distinction of seasons

There was that time at your parents'
I couldn't pass for a man
Slurring my words like a second language
It drizzled on the Fourth of July
They loved me before that moment
I can't recall if they said goodbye

And I poured a glass this evening
Red wine from a dusty bottle
Dinner for one, just me, myself, and I
And my reflection in the glass was my date
The very first sip made me gag
Left the rest and went to stand outside

I miss the springs we had
With our friends in the outdoor bar
Rustic roof for when times were gloomy
Pregnant clouds above us
Rainfall reminds you to cherish
Never take for granted the sun

I took for the granted the morning mist
It clouded the ineffable inevitable dawn
The mornings I woke with sweat and regret
There were times I wanted to change your last name
Other times the bottle tasted too numb for shame
You do not know misery like I do.

So actually, usually, I'm not alone
I eat supper these days with Channel 9
Weatherman's a friend of mine
Don't know each other's names
But he's always honest to me
And we're both always on time

I'm sorry for the way things ended
Caught up in the moment I was scared of the end
I didn't want to face you
But I see your face in the sun-streaked sky
The dying red gives light to look back on the day
There's beauty in finality don't you think?

I didn't watch the weather tonight
I stood up my only friend left
And he could've mentioned the end of the world
Could've said that tonight was the last one to come
But it wouldn't change my evening thoughts
Stars fall from the sky to shine on my face

'Cause something today sparked my interest
I'm intrigued about you and the meaning of life
Suddenly I inhale the clarity of sight
I'm in love with chaos and joy and the drops of dew
I wanna be sober for the end of the world
And I wanna be with you

That Liberating Feeling of Nonsense
(a tale about divorce)

She flew shaking sky low
Hebrews taking Shiloh
Battle, chains, gray-blue, bold, and red
Cattle slain, stay true, golden, dead
Cherubim halo glowing light
Marry him, stay low, knowing night

Bull Run rise, giants' known fall
Fulcrum cries, silent stonewall
Bridesmaids violet virgin veil
Sighed, stayed high, let her sin fail
Quest for shoes, sword feather grim Picket
Restless Jews horde Rephidim Spigot

Lee, trenches, Appomattox
Sea drenches Captain Haddock's
Promised Land, Azreal's wings
Mom insist band jazz she'll sing
But this kid knows deeper blues
Slut kiss, widows see virtues

I do- I don't, abusive fuck
Shy too, cry won't ya, lose, live stuck
Better dead than the decay to you
"Let her," said Grandpa, "Betray you too."
Fiat passed, she scat fast
Free at last, free at last

I Breathe to Life the Southern Wind

I hear the heartbeat slowing down
I watch the eaves from green to brown
Paschal angels so feared I lost her
A whistle through the valley bring
Like dying stories of a fabled king
Seventh week from the Reign of Auster

So comes the northern wind to blow
Leaves wet and cold from rain and snow
I don't really know what I feel these days
Summer affair beyond its due
The first month we've had that wasn't new
The southern wind comes but never stays

Not so sober in the grocery store
Making fun of the couple next door
Bonfire pallets on New Year's Day
Has the northern wind put us to smoke?
With not so much as an ember to poke?
Fragile autumn leaf decay

Whispers in the city square
See I never claimed that life was fair
But I thought we'd survive another fall
With the evening solstice drawing near
I cannot let you go my dear
Deaf to the reaper of seasons's call

'Cause our season is here to stay
You and I won't just fade away
The southern wind is out of breath
But I've air in my lungs that won't deflate
So I'll bring it to life, resuscitate
And bring our romance up from death

Black Mass

Holy man once was I
Until you caught my lustful eye
Now I conjure marital lies
Communion with the lord of the flies

Wife's spouse thou doth covet
Consecrate this unholy coven
Certain devil of a husband
Doing deeds we verily mustn't

These days I hiss at holy water
To blame because 'twas I who sought her
Laying in bed with satan's daughter
This hell we've made is getting hotter

The exhilaration of the dark abyss
You and I and Asmodeus
My bride at home in ignorant bliss
Return each night with judas kiss

Lay thee on this altar
Feel my conscience falter

Feel thy body rise like yeast
Sign ourselves, mark of the best

Idol in my palms
Hymning backwards psalms

Transgression and possession

Consummation, levitation

Trace thy body numb.
Two fingers and a thumb.
Make thy kingdom come.
What one earth have I become?

Prescription

Slip it in and do it quickly
Stress the vein and hold it down
Inject it deep within me
I don't want to feel this now

Just push a little more now
Empty the syringe
And maybe they'll all cease to howl
Before they even begin

Open up the lid and
Pour it upside down
Swallow every pill and gram
Make these memories drown

Drain the flask completely
I don't want to see a drop
Make sure the bottle's empty
Maybe then they'll stop

Press your foot upon the spade
Into the cold, hard ground
Until the hole is made
Bury it deep down

Hold your ears and close your eyes
Sing something in your head
Until the memory dies
Make them all stay dead
But it's only a matter of time
The flashbacks still will start
They'll run rampant through my mind
They'll start clawing at my heart

See I know what I could give her
Ad that my love was true
But the woman loves another
And I am left to view
So please inject it all now
Push the needle fully in
Let these wicked feelings drown
In pain and medicine

But solution it is lacking
Because I can see her eyes
She's concerned about my actions
But she cannot fathom why

The Foolishness of Daedalus

When I was just a child my father warned me stern

You are my joy and pride my boy
If you get the chance to dance
To fly so high up in the sky

At a ball to twirl and fall for a girl
She'll give light so bright it costs your sight
Promise me son avoid the sun

She'll leave you with a burn

Where the Lightning Lands

[I]
Looking down at the ground from 22D
Through clouds and around at 40,000 feet
The distance, I witnessed a spark in the sky
It was lightning brightening up my eye
An engine stall brought freefall, I forgot to breathe
A second later we were safer but to no relief

[II]
2017 in between a casket and a pew
I say goodbye as bagpipes cry a somber highland tune
Letting go of Uncle Co was an aching pain
Stepped outside, buried with pride, coffin in the rain
Three-gun salute rang out mute from tremble up above
Flash so bright, moment of light, then back to lack thereof

[III]
Tales of old of pots of gold at the end of the rainbow
But what is under that bolt of thunder- curious what's below
Everyone hears what disappears to split the stately trees
And homing rods catch darts from gods but no one truly sees
All my years my covered ears sought the final place
Where lightning lands- now I understand

It illuminates your face

Wandering Star

I'm just a goodtime girl flying through the cosmic void
All my life I've always been a voyaging asteroid

Astronomers have studied me but all their theories fail
I'm clearly not a comet- I don't even have a tail

Glance up to the heavens and see that shooting star
I'm every constellation that has ever been in art

And stories build around me of my beauty and my hue
I've seen everything that fusion brings- that was 'till I saw you

I've passed through solar systems and left without a trace
But recently I'm lonely 'cause there is no sound in space

I just circle 'round your atmosphere until I cannot breathe
Pulled down by a gravity I cannot seem to leave

I rotate as I orbit, show you my dark side
You just giggle when you see it, and offer me your tide

I don't want to be your star, I don't want to be your moon
So pull me down from Heaven, and boy please do it soon

I am not scared to burn out as I approach your face
I wanna make my crater next to you for all my days

Age Gap

I'm too old for you
Please don't ask

What's the difference between you and me?
Twenty five and twenty three?
My years just had more density

I've already lived a full life
Climax and falling action

Time heal scars but scars add years
Sewing division between me and my peers

You're a warm rising wind new to convection
All your life you've blown where you've pleased
But I am weathered

Dreaming in Parallel

Featuring Al and Sue

My blinds are made of open slits
They beckon the pale moonbeams to split
Light in patterns upon my face
Dreaming here of my fall from grace
Once I was a star, up so high
Twinkle twinkle within his eye
But now his mind contains me not
I don't reside in a single thought

Our mutual friends avoid his name
And they try to pretend it's all the same
And it is for him, my parallel friend
Whisper his name, my heart to rend
I try and try, not to stalk him online
I cry and cry, when I see he's just fine
How did I make this horrific mistake
Which was the dream? Am I awake?

Silly girl I was, dreaming of a ring

Next weekend is All Souls' Day
A year's been given and taken away
And I'm not sure what it means anymore
And I only feel like a fucking whore
Cause what is my body, if not hers?
The hell am I Sue, if not yours?
What did it mean? I thought we'd last
I swore our future would be my past

Memories linger just out of sight
What does she dream in October nights?
What does she think when she does her hair?
Does look for me in the autumn air?
Almost a year and what have I done?
There's nothing new under the sun
Will I be haunted forever by you?
On the cusp of my eyes, just out of view?

Stupid boy I was, losing everything

White Picket Pipedream

Done with that recent shorty
She took it kinda poorly

Said some things I do not care
Tossed around a slur, a swear

Said I used her just for sex
So I just pressed that little x

I don't think I'm in the wrong
Couldn't stick around for long

She was pretty chill at first
Tho kinda turned into the worst

Guess that I'm onto the next
Ignore her future late-night text

So here am I daydreaming
Struggling for meaning

Not much to do, a lazy day
High on my couch that hazy way

What to say? They come and go
Is there an end? I do not know

I think about my deadbeat dad
I think about my mother sad

What about Unc and his own
Married for years and never alone

Is that a thing, that Hollywood feel?
Is that even something real?

That wife and grandkids on the swing
Are there females worth a ring?

I'm sick of games but could I win?
Or is that just church invention?

I'll bug Unc for advice, no beaming
But for now just keep day-dreaming

Consistency

Tonight I'm enveloped in your grace
I feel the warmth of your embrace
And you're all mine
All mine

There's a voice crying deep inside
But it doesn't fight it only hides
Stick up for yourself!
This time!

But again I have your affection
Your touch and its affliction
Hold me close
You kiss back

The uncertain sun will rise tomorrow
Because you only seek to borrow
But keep me!
Retain me

But tonight you are mine
All mine

Beneath the Badland Moon

How many shades of white
A crescent above my eye
And a billion stars piercing through clouds

How many shades of black
An outstretched canvas sky
And a billion pockets of enticing darkness

There's a gentle whisper
I hear it through the sage tonight
Whispers of desperate wildlife

Shadows of mountains lord over horizon
There could I be safe?
There are no lions in the badlands

But the dirt against my back is cold
Tonight I did not loose a rope
The rattlesnakes are hibernating

I am alone this barren night
Alone except for my old friend Shoe
Shoe the mule of ample stride

I used to have a pony
A gift from the Shoshone
But the prairie dogs conspired

Shoe the mule of ample step
My family tree will continue as his
Shoe is a mule, the brother of my Colt

Colt's steel is cold against my skin
Splintered wood by the inscription
Colt, the brother of mule, brother of mine

I wish I had another coat
Some leather dried upon my side
While leaning on ponderosa hide

How many shades

PART

II

NEWS FROM THE FRONT
OF THE WAR OF POETRY

In a world governed by the unhuman powers of hell, who seek to reduce us to our animalistic ways, who cannot comprehend things like empathy or humility, music or moon landings, architecture or art, symphonies or superbowls, being human is a declaration of rebellion.

And poetry is an act of warfare.

So join me, as we embark upon the warpath against pretty girls flaunting 9th Grade poetry, the confounding mysteries of the human experience, and all the gods in high places.

The Death of Poetry

More than a maiden is Poetry
The sought-after lady, Eurydice

Disheartening to see her brought asunder
All of her spoils taken for plunder

Girls with nothing but pretty faces
Reading trash with theatrical graces

Pretentious one-liners surrounded by fluff
I cannot express how I'm sick of the stuff

I fear my wife to be taken by Hades
I weep and I mourn the fairest of ladies

My lyre in hand and my rhymes well-fed
Watch me raise her up from the dead

Guillotine

So loyal since your Nashville debut
Arguments fought in defense over you

But your self-proclaimed title brings me dismay
Chairman of poets? That's not very slay

A letter of grievance to the chairman herself
Take that accolade off of your shelf

We've fashioned into a molten calf
But woman please, cut your ego in half

Watch me slowly increase my meter
It works without using my voice- ya lil cheater

See I love ghostly lyrics mixing heartbreak and fears
So you had me going with ricocheted tears

But you lost me with that line about battleships
It shadows your verse's shine with eclipse

It's like the only rhyme you could think of was sinking waves
But it loses the theme and you should've used "graves"

18 years since we first heard your sound
Yet multi-syllable rhymes still unfound

Your voice can put hearts into a chokehold
But convey your tone through syntax not vocals

I could really get past the rest of it all
But arrogant tyrants deserve a fall

So I'm no longer loyal to my queen
I come to you dragging a guillotine

Writer's Block

(An ode to the art)

~~~

You know me well you know my trade
I write about things with rhythm and rhyme
But lately something has got me irate
Curious feelings for this girl of mine

I tried to write a poem for her last eve
A gift for 6 months since our eyes first locked
But the funniest thing you wouldn't believe
My mind is blank- I've got writer's block

~~~

So I cried frustrated o'er pride, lust, hatred
Four more demons screamin' find-the-rhyme

Hand me my pencil, and see I then will
Then will- I will- I
Backspace- er jeeze it's dead
Pass eraser please instead

~~~

I can write words in a manner that's art
I promised a poem for her alone
But now I don't even know where to start
Like what even are syntax and tone?

I cannot believe I cannot write
Self-imposed deadline mere hours away
I already booked us dinner tonight
Flowers or jewelry would just be cliche

~~~

On the topic of flowers I'm predisposed
It's nearly entropic how her laugh is rose
Panned gold gleams with pressured coal
But her handhold means my rest assured soul

I've always, as a boy, held courage dear
My tall ways destroyed with divergent fear

A small thing scarier is my falling barrier from
my temple's steeple tall above

My inferior self-interior once protected now reflected
from green irises while injected and infected by
unseen viruses like the one people call love

~~~

I'll just have to write her something new
Some simple lines to keep her amused
A meter cheap and quick
A dandy limerick
Or perhaps I'll gift her a haiku

But haikus are too
Short and complete thoughts should not
Spill past lines to rhyme

Rhymes themselves are difficult to contrive
From dust we breathe clay golems alive
Music in songs blends sounds together
It fastens near-rhymes into seamless leather
But poetry naked lacks this disguise
Its veil is transparent and permits no lies

~~~

I think I suppose that's her barren appeal
My shrink's prescribed dose hides what's real
That was okay but she's such a light to see
Spat the clay, rub these eyes, return sight to me

Insecurities reckon my failure to rise
But no perjuries beckon her compromise
The world sees my girl as ever she is
A beauty for to see, that's never specious

~~~

I just want this poem to make her smile
But (annunciate fully) it's just futile
Attempts all crumpled up in vain
Second-hand's subtle tick in my brain

Words are oil I must be water
Brew or boil I'm steaming hotter
Words, lexicon it once came easy
Perplexed sonneteer ashamed and measly

Maybe my words don't have to rhyme
Great poets do as such all the time

Write some freeform lines to read her
A favor to ask if you'd be so kind
Keep time for me and count my meter?

~~~

The truth is that maybe I'm a little scared
It's only been six months and things are moving fast
I've always felt six stories high but she's a skyscraper
No, she's the whole skyline and I see sunsets refracted
-by all the windows of her compound eyes

I'd like to imagine her lips are the same shade of crimson as my heart
My hands are heavier empty than when they're holding hers
She teases that she stole my hoodie
But with 4 coats on I'm still naked without her embrace

Naked
Opened for all the world to see
But what if she opens me up like a treasure chest?
Will she be disappointed when she sees nothing but cobwebs?

And will skyscrapers fall with clouds of dust around her?
When she realizes that I don't deserve the view she offers?
Will all the crimson be drained from her lips?
Drained by the sun as it sets on us?
And will I choke when all the dust around us settles?
Even now my heart skips a beat when I
Wait
Hold on just a second

That wasn't my heart, that skipped a beat or two
No, that was my rhythm and my meter too
I asked you to keep time for me
For a confidante you're pretty lousy

~~~

But if not you then whom?
And if not me then my white plume?
And if not now then when to bloom?
Sealed away in a marble tomb
Six feet into the earth's cold womb
I write this poem or sign my doom

Damned if I do damned if I don't
Saved if I can but I know that I won't
Feelings for her I can't describe
Damned if I can't get my hand to scribe

Dependent on nothing but hubris high
Pendulum on a string- cut through this lie
Grandfather still taunts me tick tock tick
Hand's orbital's sinusoidal, periodic
And it's ternary, constantly metronomic

Cerebral tissue leaks from my ears
Terrible issue speaks and I hear
Thoughts and thoughts- scramble about
Brought and wrought (violence and doubt)
Some tell me this woman I can't afford
Compels me to measure the things I've stored
Voices elsewhere decry and detest
Choices well made, see I am the best

Coronate me king of poetry on a throne
Born late it's Poe yet he died alone
Lines blend between formulae and art
Heightened by my oscillating heart
Find loopholes for rules that don't even exist
Paradoxical parallel lines with clean nexus
Like rhyming couplets with vivid end
Syllable count means squat if the rhyme serves its dividend

Ascending this daunting jagged height
The ending is vaunting ragged pride
Creeping closer the tiptoe of fate
Peeping over the window of late
The fuse approaches its unburnt end
The muse encroaches its run cur-tain
Maybe something yet will come!
Another hour is all I want!

—Alarm rings out six o'clock on the dot
Time for our date, let's see what I got
Look down on my paper at the fatal hark
Nothing but ego
And eraser marks

~~~~~~

So come one and all to lend me your aid
Show unto me the art of my trade

I wrote nay I smote with deitivity in past
My rhymes my divine creativity have lapsed

Swear to be careful; it's quite a shock
There is no peril like writer's block

into that good night

The black desert canvas is static
But the stars it suspends are aching
They pull at the strings of their marionette
Ready to streak down like buzzing rain
Yearning to touch down on barren sand
To bring blazing light to the sterile earth

The highway stretches onward
Reaching a place their light dares not

...

Oh say can you see by the beams of my brights
A dark sign made green by the soft touch of light
307 miles to the silk ribbon
I can get there by moonset

Every gas stop is vacant at 3am
No coffee to boost my adrenaline
But my eyelids are light and my mind's far from idle
Kept awake by angelsong

Thinking back on the ides of August
Harvest shades in her glistening eyes
College for her and I meant four years apart
In hindsight we were naive

In foresight is my dashboard
Live readings from my trash Ford
Wheels of fate churn at the RPM
I smash the odometer

Cause fuck it

The distance and time just beat us down
But I've stood in the ring round after round
I've held on tight to that bloody rope
Against all odds and against all hope

She's held out too but she's losing strength
So I launched this voyage great in length
Her phone calls short and emotionless
Her friend warned me of a guy named Wes

The air around me is suddenly alive
So I roll down the windows at 85
Celestial operas offering laud
Creation is shouting the glory of God

I can no longer discern the engine's hum
As the chants of the angels converge into one
And the desert ensemble begins to rise
The anthem approaches unparalleled highs

Destiny beckons me in my plight
Rage, rage against the dying of night
Cannot, will not, stop to rest
Cannot halt this urgent quest
Cannot, will not, miss
It all leads to this
Wind in sail
Will avail

Persevere against all strife
That girl's the love of my life

Headfray

Zulu cries and heads held high
Do you remember fighting the sky
We'd beat it down with sticks as swords
Creed and street honor our reward
Recall skipping over sidewalk cracks
Freefall tripping for our mothers' backs
Battle-born scars exalted by band aids
Adderall, scorned, and lands unflayed
What a time to be alive
Yet the two of us were barely five

And do you remember the love of my life
Hand through hand holding a knife
She was a fighter like you and I
Free us from her vows, her lies
I do, my first and final breath
Cry anew may part do us death
Finding love again and climbing K2
Writing about things I'll never do
Blues talking about things my mind can't get through
Jews walking on water and lies told by you

Plague on both your houses
Vague intentions, bleeding callouses
Oldest, longest, former friend
Hold best, wrong I guess, brothers to the end
And heart and mind and flesh at war
Ramparts covered in blood and more
Carving the sky, cutting down stars
Marveling at the conflict near and far
My friend and lover found to frivol
I can promise this war will not be civil

Secular though I have become still
Insecure enough to kill an angel
So many chemicals and pathways at play
So lend me a bottle of pills and I'll pray
Attention deficit to manic depression
Retention of hyperactive expression
Caught in the crossfire trying to stay neutral
Wrought to feel a pulse, barely fruitful
Land mines and trenches and chaos ensues
Clandestine struggle enclosed from all view

PART

III

to the ones who keep
their stories untold

Daddy's on the Moon

My daddy is a spaceman
He flies rocket ships through space
And he wears a funny helmet and suit
And he eats some special dried-out fruit
We were so excited when he left last week
To go up there so high

My daddy's on the moon
That's what my mommy says
She says he's up above
Watching me with a heart full of love
So whenever I go to sleep at night
If I see the moon my daddy sees me

He's up amongst the stars she says
Thinking always and only about me
Shining in the dark night sky
So when I miss him I don't have to cry
My mother says he called in fact
He's sorry he missed my first ballet

I never have to miss him
I never have to be sad
My mother says he's watching me always
And that in his heart my memory stays
But I wish she wouldn't lie to me
I know the shuttle went down

I can watch the tv
And I can read the news
I wish she wouldn't tell me these lies
When I know my daddy went and died
He'll never talk to me again
And I'll never again hold his hand

But tonight when my mommy tucks me in
And asks me to wish my daddy sweet dreams
I'll peak out the blinds at the only light
And pretend to wish him a good goodnight
And then I'll sleep and think of him
And dream that my daddy's on the moon

Bleak

I fell asleep on the couch last night
It's become a habit now
Without a blanket the leather is cold
And all I want to do is hold
Hold the thing on the other side of the wall
Sleeping in our queen sized bed

I remember the first time I fell in love
I say first, it happens every day
Recall that night at our friends' little shack
Sitting beside the fire out back
We'd been together for a year by then
I'm surprised it took me so long

I asked her to marry me within a year
And she said yes cause she loved me
So our loved ones formed a crowd
I lifter her veil and we both vowed
I swear I meant those words
The bad times are here

It was a year ago we lost Matthew
That's the name she decided
She buried our baby in a little grave
For her I will always be strong and brave
She'll never know that I'm weak too
I visit my stillborn boy every week to cry

It was two months ago when I got laid off
Since the money quit coming in
There wasn't much to start
We saved a little, we were smart
It's not too bad yet
But I can't find a job and fear's creeping in

It was three nights ago when I saw it
I told her not to be scared
We'd survive when push came to shove
We'd endure because we were in love
But when I looked in her eyes I knew
I knew it was a lie at least for her

I love her more and more each day
My beautiful bride my beautiful wife
But I know she doesn't love me anymore
I was excited for what marriage had in store
I was excited for every second
And I fall in love with her every second

And every second I lose her more
All this time I thought love was mutual
The contrast of permanence to lack thereof
How does one person fall out of love
As the other falls madly and desperately
Into the deepest of highs

Proposal

("A poem about two strangers and a little ring")

I walk down the empty aisle
Past all these empty pews
As tears build up inside
All I see is you

You're waiting at the altar
As beautiful ever
My recent dreams have been
Of you and I forever

My hand brushes my pocket
I feel the silver ring
Without you by my side
This world won't mean a thing

I stand before you now
It suddenly dawns on me
That everything is backwards
This isn't how it's s'pposed to be

You should've been the one
To walk down all these rows
All eyes upon your dress
Why'd you have to go?

I look down upon your casket
As a tear rolls down my eye
We were gonna be forever
You weren't supposed to die

I drop down on one knee
Draw forth the silver band
I slip it on your finger
Forever hold your hand

The Ballad of the Bullets

Have you ever heard a melody
A sound so unexplained
A sound from God knows where
I've heard the harps of cherubim
The faintest song of whizzing air

Helmet netting wet on my hair
And cold trench against my back
Notes all around, boundless and free
Instruments I cannot recognize
Such that seem so innate to me

Recollect from when I was young
Mother took me to the theatre
But of all the operas hummed along
Of all the symphonies ever played
The shearing of air is an unknown song

Neither poetic nor romantic
Not superfluous at all
Onomatopoeia of a foreign tongue
A language known yet not by man
A hymn unhummed, a song unsung

It doesn't sound like my ideals
It doesn't even sound like death
Nor what I am fighting for
It's not the sound of sacrifice
It's just the constant sound of war

The ballad of these tearing rounds
This orchestra of speed and wind
The soliloquy of thick air shred
I don't dislike or enjoy it but know
For all my life, to be stuck in my head

Baby Shower

I'm just shy of a whimper
I've never felt so small
I can't create a whisper
I can't create at all

Please, you must believe me
Never thought I'd be this girl
But things just rushed around me
I wanted to be ready
To be just like my mom

But my house of cards
Built on shifting sand
It crumpled down
All around
Cold feet cannot be helped

And I wanted so to love you
My little boy inside
But mama had to let you down
Not as strong as my own mom
Couldn't name you after my dad

And a horrid present in the mail
With ribbon and unknowing card
What to tell my mother's mom?
I had a change of heart
No grandchild for her this year

Mom must not have told her
That I couldn't follow through
Grandma's gift of baby blue
While suddenly I have the blues
Clutching a pair of baby shoes

What's Wrong with Now?

The night regains its voices
Crickets, drizzle, and an arid breeze
Winds that blow wherever you please
Confused by recent choices
She said no?

Did I pick the wrong song to sing?
Select incorrectly this ring?
She said no.

Quips and clips of things she said
They ricochet about my head
No.

Yes I meant it
We're just too young
Wait a few years
Brunch tomorrow?

Brunch is all I got with a ring
Hunch that it's not worth the sting
Still too young at seventeen?

When's the point of "maturity"?
Feels as ready as they'll ever be
So what's the reason to wait?
What's the motive to hesitate?

Standing here in silence
With the chatter of the night
She thinks nothing's changed
Stars below and fields above me
Clutching spurned jewelry

Born to be a Road Cross

This isn't a lesson only my tale
Only my canticle of ethereal dusk
Gothic prophecy over my cradle
I was marked among others from dawn
A Chosen One for inheritance fatal
Listen to my whisper of silence made whole

Sang along with Schultz
I was not born to drown
But I shan't recall that melody
Not six feet underground

Now the only song I know is this

Celebrate life in tender seasons
In the infant springtime I first cried
My autumn heart to render reasons
Winter sirens called from roadside

I heard my name in the rumble strip

A plethora of words rush by you
My peripheral biography
You focus on the road

Don't blame the driver for spilling his drink
Fault to the Fates for snipping my string
Fault to the angels for singing my name
Fault to the heavens, Heaven's to blame

Humans are stardust a wonderful saying
Scatter mine or I'll rust where I'm laying
Humans are profit, destined for loss
Some for parents, and others kings
I was born to be a road cross

Guardian Angel

Dedicated to the heroic exploits of Mr. Little, and to all his comrades easing turbulent hearts with gentile purrs

It's only a cat
It's only a cat
A bundle of furs and purrs
And little pokey whiskers

It's only a cat
Tho let me admit
It saved me from my own hand
On the edge of my rope
(Tied in a noose)
I couldn't go thru with it
Because I had a cat

The gentlest of kittens
The gentleman himself
No scars levied on me from ghosts of past
Nothing in that moment
Nothing worth more than that cat

It's only a cat
Yeah I know it's true
But he's never left me
Most unlike you
And he's never hurt me
(Except for a scratch)
Most unlike you

But this poem is not about you
It's about little old me who once was blue
And how I survived an inch from my life
When it would've been easy from life to scat
My life is in debt to this little cat

(but he's not so little anymore)